World Without End

CLAUDE WILKINSON

World Without End

Poems

SLANT
BOOKS

WORLD WITHOUT END
Poems

Copyright © 2020 Claude Wilkinson. All rights reserved. Except for brief quotations in critical publications or reviews, no part of this book may be reproduced in any manner without prior written permission from the publisher. Write: Permissions, Slant Books P.O. Box 60295, Seattle, WA 98160.

Slant Books
P.O. Box 60295
Seattle, WA 98160

www.slantbooks.com

PAPERBACK ISBN: 978-1-63982-036-8
HARDCOVER ISBN: 978-1-63982-037-5
EBOOK ISBN: 978-1-63982-038-2

Cataloguing-in-Publication data:

Names: Wilkinson, Claude.

Title: World without end : poems / Claude Wilkinson.

Description: Seattle, WA: Slant Books, 2020.

Identifiers: ISBN 978-1-63982-036-8 (paperback) | ISBN 978-1-63982-037-5 (hardcover) | ISBN 978-1-63982-038-2 (ebook)

Subjects: LCSH: American poetry | Poets, American | POETRY—American—African American | American poetry—21st century

Classification: PS3573.I44183 W675 2020 (print) | PS3573.I44183 (ebook)

Manufactured in the U.S.A.   10/07/21

Evening passed and morning came—that was the first day.

—Genesis 1:5

The first poetry is always written against the wind by sailors and farmers who sing with the wind in their teeth. The second poetry is written by scholars and students, wine drinkers who have learned to know a good thing. The third poetry is sometimes never written; but when it is, it is written by those who have brought nature and art together into one thing.

—Walter Inglis Anderson

Contents

I
Among Other Things, My Father Teaches Me How to Mow Grass | 2
Four-leaf Clovers in Bibles | 3
A Flight of Doves for Sherley Guy | 5
Auspice | 7
Eclipse | 8
Heaven and Earth | 11
Salvia | 13
Lenten | 15
Remembering My Mother Cleaning Fish | 17
Snow | 18

II
Covenant | 22
A Fledgling Ornithologist Attempts to Explain the Difference between Birds and Angels | 23
Praise | 25
Watching a Rosarian Prune Canes | 27
Sunday Morning Wildflowers | 29
Driving Home While Thinking of a Sermon I Had Just Heard on How God Even Looks After All the Animals Too When a Butterfly Collides with My Car's Windshield | 31
Prophecy | 33
Psalm | 35

III
In the Beginning, Audubon | 38

Theodore Dreiser Watches a Lobster Kill a Squid
in an Aquarium | 39

Rumiesque Perhaps | 40

Walter Anderson Regrets Killing
a Sea Turtle | 41

Theories on How Venus de Milo
Lost Her Arms | 43

Vincent's Flowers | 44

IV

Weed | 54

Wasps | 56

A Guide for Listening to Mockingbirds | 57

The Love Life of Moss | 59

Flower Moon | 60

Internecine | 61

Destroying Angel | 63

Duet | 64

Dragonflies Hunting | 65

Live Bait | 66

Cottonmouth | 68

Montego Bay | 69

The Goliath Bird-Eating Spider | 71

The Mud Dauber and the Moth | 72

A Hunter with a 23½-Pound Wild Turkey Heads
toward His Boat Near Big Island on the Mississippi River | 74

Deer Crossing | 75

Thusness | 77

Forecast | 78

Revelation | 79

Winter Field White with Snow Geese | 81

World Without End | 83

Acknowledgments | 85

I

AMONG OTHER THINGS, MY FATHER TEACHES ME HOW TO MOW GRASS

Of course, there would be further nuggets,
such as keeping my hands at ten and two o'clock
around the Polara's big steering wheel,
that girls could easily get pregnant,
but first, it was his way to steady a lawn mower
with a foot on top before snatching the starter rope,
as I now imagine Nimrod might have taught his son
how to draw a bow. Never mind Mississippi heat—
anytime after the dew had dried and grass
was over two inches tall, a yard was fit to be cut.
And if, for any reason, it wasn't finished before dusk,
I could still go on under light of our rural moon
as long as I held to his simple rules:
whether you are a child too close to your world,
merely trust the brilliant lizard
will skitter to safety; don't get distracted
by a mist of whiteflies who burst up before you
like petals off windblown violets;
and though you see them with complete adoration,
expect even grounded lightning bugs
to fend for themselves; last, yet above all else,
after making that first straight pass, be sure
the mower's inside wheels roll in your outside track
so the side discharge blows clippings away
from the part you've already cut, which I
then tried to take as a kind of blessed assurance
that everything in this life, if done
just right, should somehow fall in place.

FOUR-LEAF CLOVERS IN BIBLES

As with teacakes and cloudlike meringues,
in this too, my mother was expert.
Under a net of evening shade
from our two huge walnut trees,
she would sit on her old wrought-iron chair
in the hush just after supper swatting sweat bees
and pointing me in the right direction.

Among scents of wild allium
and waves of green deception,
I groped from cold to closer
to there at my sweeping palm
where were clustered three or more
of the magic charms she had seen
at least six feet away.

A whole minute might go by
as she twirled them between
her index finger and thumb
as if checking genuineness
before sending me for her Bible
with the white leather cover
and luminous Sacré-Coeur
stung with a ring of thorns
above its table of contents.

Somewhere after the Fall
but before the Resurrection, her favor
ripened from emerald to golden
in columns like verses themselves
amid Job's patience or Solomon's wisdom.

The first leaf, they say, bears hope;
the second, ironically, faith;
the third leaf is for love,
and a fourth holds the luck.
When there's a fifth, even a sixth,
they are paths to money and fame.
And if ever a seventh, the finder
can count on a long life as well.

Though our chances at nature's lottery
are figured to be only one
in ten thousand, or half those odds,
if you believe the optimists.

Still, they were hunted then harbored
in Bibles of other women
in the community too, as they had been
by their mothers and so on,
perhaps for happier marriages,
better children, or a bountiful garden.

On occasion, when I spot their fortunes now
while spraying anthills or weeding the lawn,
I sometimes imagine an endless line
of all the saintly others, like my mother,
halt from worn-out knees,
taken in their dances with cancer,
going one by one through Heaven's
narrow gate, their winning bets below
perfectly hedged and pressed.

A FLIGHT OF DOVES FOR SHERLEY GUY

Beautiful clichés declare
    you're still with us in each rustling breeze,
        in "the swift, uplifting rush of quiet birds

in circling flight," that we should
    look for you now in rainbows
        instead of sweating over a hot stove

to feed the Sunday multitudes,
    that God called you this time
        rather than another community family

needing your help with one
    of their sick, that you've found rest
        at last from peddling your produce

for a cache of bosom money
    O donor of silver dollars through generations
        of adoring children, rest even for you, O patron saint

of suspending your widow's work
    and offering any of at least five leftover desserts
        to every visitor who dropped by,

that your reticent mirth
    when remembering a gluttonous cousin
        or some wisp of gossip, which you were usually

too good to tell, from now on will only be
    available as "the diamond glint on snow"
        and in "gentle autumn rain." But back to the birds

    circling in flight, as did a trinity
        of milk-white doves as well as one dyed pink
            to symbolize your neophyte soul.

Meant to be the last of a fitting eulogy,
        the doves spiral higher and higher, faster,
            slower, then faster again when you've caught up

with the veteran angels,
        while I surely hear you chuckle and say,
            "I know that ain't me, I ain't never moved that fast,"

as over a distant curtain of redbuds
        in bloom, the band of wings dip from
            flawless blue sky, their ugliness astonishing.

AUSPICE

On just another day when
I already felt like shit,
through the gray drizzle, I saw
on my neighbor's magnolia
some glad little warbler
choosing the wife of his dreams,
plying her favors with a constant nectar
of insects until I thought of two girls—
either of whom maybe I should've married—
one of them long dead
and the other one now dying.

Yet there was the tide of vetch
that I had let take the yard again
this spring, and also my fears
of any number of other things
over which we might've quarreled
to no end, such as my forgetting
to bring flowers home often enough,
her calling my poems "cute,"
or I wanting us to fly
to Cape Cod for the summer,
but she preferring Pine Bluff.

ECLIPSE

I

Among the sheer oversimplifications
are tools used as proofs,
such as marbles, a flashlight,
and different-sized balls, so that
each brightness that was let be
to rule day and night can be had
from most five-and-dimes.

Credits are dredged up
for everything surrounding it—
first, for the ancient Chaldeans,
who, despite biblical tales of ineptness
at discerning Nebuchadnezzar's dream,
somehow apprehended enough
of the mystery of the heavens
to learn the saros, or repetition
of eclipses' occurrence.

Celebrity is bandied about,
Einstein being mentioned
for particulars to do with gravity,
and Olaus Roemer, who
while gazing at Jupiter's obscuring,
claimed the proximate speed of light.

Almost as if an apology, we're told
that they were once, *once* mind you,
thought to be miracles, possibly similar
to a late summer meadow's

pulsing fireflies or the pod of bluest whales
breaching an ocean's constant thunder.

There's no room now for musing
on some brief dalliance
between Diana and Apollo,
since our astronomers
have become so precise.
Yet even after
hard science explanations,
what remains is still
always called "beautiful," always
"the beautiful corona."

2

But what could any of this mean
when a cousin has been lost
just a few days before, with whom
I played stickball as a kid
and was bound with
in the same middle age.

Compared to throngs of those awaiting
their phenomenon of cosmic luck,
while for others, this wondrous death
and resurrection of the sun, few gathered
at a highway funeral home
to witness what it's like
when a man who was conceived
and was born, lived, worked,
and married, who had children
and grandchildren of his own,

who was both diagnosed
and treated with a sort of poison,
and was then at last,

in a moment, wholly
overtaken and overshadowed
by his small disease.

HEAVEN AND EARTH

Some days bluebirds are too much
    from God, as when one lit in the frill

of Queen Anne's lace, for a holy moment
    looked straight to my eyes in the tongues

of angels and of men without ever singing a note—
    his rust-colored breast a parable of terra firma,

the wound of our constant condition.
    So yes, I thought of a friend trembling

under Parkinson's, who can no longer
    even hold his camera steady he tells me,

how he's up to over twenty different pills a day.
    Once, maybe two or three years back,

we talked about what an art form
    bagging groceries used to be, how even

the greenest teenagers knew to separate
    canned goods from fruit—all to underscore,

in our now middle-aged way of looking
    at things, the downward spiral our world is on.

And yes, I thought of Maeterlinck's play *L'Oiseau bleu*,
    its morality of pedestrian happiness,

such as having virtue and every night
    seeing that the stars are still present.

Only where is our guide, our Bérylune to say
    what is or isn't fair? Then just as suddenly,

the little fellow hopped a perfect half-pirouette
    for me to behold the fullness of his glory

and every answer there in that satin firmament.

SALVIA

If this was to be the last time,
    we both must have thought, *let it be bright!*

when we decided to fill the spaces
    between his bank of pines lining the roadside.

Mostly that season we would pass the easier, muted beauty
    of something like lemon drops

for the pow-pictures of gloriosa daisies, bee balm,
    or a fringe of chrysanthemums.

Then there were the cartons of salvia,
    radiant as blood and already in bloom,

under a tableau of foreign horticultural matter
    telling us of opposite leaves and two-lipped corolla.

Family and tribe names of *Lamiaceae* and *Mentheae*
    towered as mythic gods above our pronunciation.

Excepting a green thumb, everything else
    one might ask for was there about their bracts

and racemes, the bell-shaped calyx.
    For the moment, we would resist our knowledge

that they wouldn't get full sun,
    loamy, well-drained soil, or the deadheading

they occasionally needed. After all, how long
    could any of this possibly last

beyond the brevity of our choosing
    and finally planting flowers together.

It wasn't until many years later, during a snowy winter day's
    cacophony of grackles, and since my old man's

good-byes of a sort, as I was imagining
    some remedy of brightness for my own yard,

recalling how I came to learn "salvia"
    is derived from the Latin *salvere*, which means

"to feel well" or "to heal," when I also recalled
    three seemingly disparate sentences

that I'd once seen translated from Sanskrit
    saying, "Two crows dwell in a tree"; "The God speaks";

and "Why does the son not remember the father?"

LENTEN

Like this one, many a Sunday morning
I've wondered if it wouldn't have been better
to be a supposed soulless form of life—
say, with a rabbit's liberty, at least springing
toward some obvious purpose of timothy or clover
greening through our surprise snow in March,
even either of two robins squabbling
for a crab apple perch—that is,
till I remember a dooming hawk
who thrones on the bustling wires,
or sometimes among high sweet gums,
how the other evening, he fell on a thing so small
and hopeless crossing a dandelion gauntlet.

Still, what it is to be always found wanting,
not entirely sold on the notion
that letting go of anything will draw one
nearer to God, at times only half believing
though this close to the cherry orchards
and dogwoods blooming, just a month out
from the full brightness of Easter.

Hardly more than a day later, I'm told
that a childhood friend has died in his sleep.
We all knew that he drank too much
and smoked too much, and had for too long,
that for quite a while there had been a blot on his lung,
but death rarely, if ever, seems a timely endeavor.

Andy Warhol, in his diary, describes it as
the ultimate embarrassment, being unable to apologize

for not returning calls and missing appointments—
as well as for the rest of us who
have to continue thinking of breakfasts,
what to put on against a new blast of cold.

They say when my friend's sister found him,
rigor mortis had begun to set in,
that in bed he was lying prostrate—the way
we might imagine Moses or Paul having done
before each one's blinding summons of light—
as if to signify that this was it: the last
and the best of what he had to give,
like a figure of the fallen Christ.

REMEMBERING MY MOTHER CLEANING FISH

How ordinary they became
in her leeching of their numb,
freshwater smell, the last
of their rainbow sheen.
Translucent scales flicked like alms
at her feet, she would then
slit the swell of their bellies
clean through to what could be
any ruffle of crimson things.

Opening a fat bullhead once,
and knowing the Bible
the way she did, my mother
more than likely thought of Jonah
when she found another whole fish inside—
in some spots above its gills
and next to fins, still as clear
as new flame, though lower,
already tinged with the rich gold
of decay—gone just long enough
to learn how infinity feels.

SNOW

If memory ever serves one correctly
    when trying to get the telling right,

I may have been alternately sharing
    my morning with Shostakovich,

The Clinch Mountain Boys,
    and Blind Lemon Jefferson's blues

pleading for his gal to drive him
    like a mule, while clouds bloomed

into expected drifts. My sister, who would come
    later, jokes that if visitors don't like my music,

all they have to do is wait a few minutes
    and it'll change completely. In the meantime,

I could've been trying to work
    some Latin into a poem, anything

to keep my mind off the moments. Now
    and then I glanced through a window

to see if something had begun, but as it does,
    it had just kept swelling in dark increments.

When my sister did come with the news
    of our mother, and this part is still as clear

as chapel bells, she said, "Mama was a good woman."

    The truth of one's order of memories doesn't matter

so much, but at some point, early on,
    I must've thought of our summer's beefy,

red tomatoes cooled with evening shade,
    beautifully sliced and plated the way she did.

When I next looked out, a last omen
    that the snowfall was ready to start

came in quiet, misty little songbirds
    out of nowhere, soon gathered about the yard.

II

COVENANT

Arcs of a double rainbow
    tie our world to violet clouds

moments before rose afterglow
    over the tops of cottonwood,

across slick lawns, again promising
    everything left will dry and be safe.

Those little olive-gold birds
    with the feathers that look

like cloisonné know it.
    Damp sparrows dipping through

passages in silvery mist
    must have also gotten a word.

Drowning here and there
    are katydids and beetles,

but there is also this remnant of music
    that's said to have once surrounded us.

And what blue morning glories,
    what full hollyhocks, and all

manner of flowers rejoicing,
    raising their heads for praise!

A FLEDGLING ORNITHOLOGIST ATTEMPTS TO EXPLAIN THE DIFFERENCE BETWEEN BIRDS AND ANGELS

She begins by mentioning Icarus
and ends by quoting Dickinson,
but those allegories aside for the moment,
she would have us believe that they too, angels
she means, are more or less corporeal
with wings ligatured at the shoulder,
which she delights "couldn't possibly get
them airborne," without the essential
"deep-keeled breastbone" which goldfinches
over eons somehow came up with themselves,
even if thanks only to earthbound enemies.

And admittedly as far as she knows,
nor do angels have "light, toothless jaws"
or the frigate bird's hollow skeleton,
that unless of the fallen kind endowed
with feasible appendages of beetles or bats,
our feathered and holy stay grounded
on feeble myth, though the psalmist David
recalls them being light and nimble enough
so that they barely ruffle the tops
of mulberry trees, though it's written one
made it all the way from empyreal heaven
well beyond the passerine, condors, or swans,
to Daniel in just twenty-one days.

Encumbered with larynges instead
of the preferred syrinx, the birdwoman offers,
neither can they ever hope to perform
a cappella amongst lilacs—something about
the division of bronchial tubes,
how the thrush can take air in
from two directions at once—thus angels'
lesser gifts of harps and lutes.
Her sorrow, for the birds she means,
is that they are caged in a world
of milliners, pillow factories, omnivores,
that her own staunch faith may be too weak
to save their miracle brilliance and melodies,
which, for her, would be hell indeed.

PRAISE

When I return home,
a cardinal chides me
from his pew
of newly green
linden leaves.

Apparently, I should've gone
to church, even on
a drizzly morning,
instead of just to market
for the bread
and blueberries
and oranges
that I needed.

For there he sits
in the heart
of his vexingly
obedient worship,
singing thanks
for his red affluence
and sound wings.

True, who can accuse him
of not always keeping
the Sabbath wholly,
but couldn't my own
ritualistic sniffing
of mangoes

and the thumping
of cantaloupes
be a similar
kind of glory?

WATCHING A ROSARIAN PRUNE CANES

There's little margin for escape when the shears
    commence their work of removing
canes that are dead or dying, any one that rubs

    against another, those
damaged by insects, storms, or disease, and those
    that are thinner than a pencil.

Maybe we could look to Darwin—you know,
    survival of the fittest,
or even further back to parables, separating

    wheat from its chaff
and all that—for one to be okay with
    such harsh condemnation.

You notice the gardener's words move
    toward ascension
when he speaks of roses' wounds yielding

    healthy growth that will
eventually bear flowers, when he says every cut
    coaxes the plant

in a certain direction, that when the bush is opened
    for air and sunlight
to flow inside, damp leaves dry quicker

    and are less likely to succumb
to harm. Not only that, but the sharpness
    of one's tools, the severity

of cuts are singled out as law. And possibly
      cruelest sounding of all
is that roses need to be "awake" before purging

      begins, so that in case
of a late freeze, a good remnant will be left.
      His every snip

is couched in terms of renewed strength,
      a perennial birth from
temporary pains. Then what we have to envision

      is tomorrow's sweet rose of Sharon,
a song's ethereal dew on petals redder than bruises,
      wholly through faith in the few

elect bud eyes. But what would a garden or anything
      else be without some association,
what need for Gethsemane without that screw-up in Eden?

SUNDAY MORNING WILDFLOWERS

The shepherd's message never took off
    or came together in any epiphanous way.

His text was from Song of Solomon,
    Mark, and James, and the title something

to the practical effect of hating
    the choice but loving the chooser.

"Certainly Lord," our choir's hymn of preparation,
    was as exalted as strange spring voices

of birds I had heard a bit earlier
    even this close to autumn and the end

of the tree frogs chirring. Though
    the hymn's question about whether our religion

is true would accept just one response,
    it had moved me only to memories

of choruses in old black and white movies
    like *The Green Pastures* and *Cabin in the Sky*,

only to a childhood when my answer felt sure.
    Of course, there were those forced moments

of solemnity in yet another's "homegoing"
    being announced, in the ritual of supping on body

and blood, and in benediction admonishing us
    to feed the sheep—again to do with love.

But before, along my way there, under
    the cumulus blue of beginning September

were sprinkled so many miracles
    of slender stems crowned with orange, pink,

yellow et cetera of poppies, lace, and daisies
    gently swaying from a cat's-paw breeze,

every flower sharing its happy ministry,
    burning with some beautiful understanding.

DRIVING HOME WHILE THINKING OF A SERMON I HAD JUST HEARD ON HOW GOD EVEN LOOKS AFTER ALL THE ANIMALS TOO WHEN A BUTTERFLY COLLIDES WITH MY CAR'S WINDSHIELD

I tried telling myself,
he had meant something
as lovely as a winter ptarmigan.
But his anecdote
was of a scruffy mutt
throughout the sweltering day,
following first one jogger
and then another in the park
until some girls who
had seen him earlier
returned to give him
shelter and water.

And though my butterfly
wasn't a monarch
with stained-glass wings,
though dusted with a duller color
like a blue-striped skipper
or Paris swallowtail,
wasn't its fragile beauty
enough for sparing,
if simply for its fragility?

Yet when I read the Bible's God
is no respecter of persons,
and remember that He who created
an elegant crane, also came up
with the hideous leech
and goofy toucan, I resign
my own notions of worthiness
to whitewashed tombs
full of dead men's bones.

PROPHECY

For the sake of record,
it's autumn, Thursday night—
anything else and the point
could be lost, if there is any
in what's more likely
just another wonder
of one's inestimable life.

But what seems important,
improbable even at harvest,
is the astonishing
storybook moon
down to the detail
of an old man's face
as close as a whisper
over burned delta fields,
their breath lingering for miles.

And then its light begins
to disappear behind an illusion
of cerulean, under a feathery
wand of cloud as it might
in a magician's trick
till nothing is left but unbelief.

If only the message
had been less ethereal,
written on the brightness
of a gilded creek, brought

as a band of unforgettable horses
stitching the rose horizon,
or even in hymns
of familiar birds.

PSALM

Just listen to the sound
of those silly bushtits singing
in spite of their pip-squeak size,
swinging on leaves, pecking their tidbits

while dangling upside down,
not mindful of Sunday morning,
of how late some of us rise
for better than spiders and aphids.

III

IN THE BEGINNING, AUDUBON

Shed of all that was Haitian
down to the sempiternal mingling

concealed in his blood,
a different quest for color

arose in the earth's kaleidoscope of birds—
one so ethereal, which he cherished

more than the others, that he couldn't
just shoot as he had the flamingos,

gyrfalcons, and quail, but rather
he limed the chalice of flowers

with honeyed wine so that
when the tiny blaze hovered in,

this one of those he called
"glittering fragments of rainbows,"

then drank till it fell from glory,
as if through a karmic prism,

spinning wings slowed to hues
from a whirring spectrum of white.

THEODORE DREISER WATCHES A LOBSTER KILL A SQUID IN AN AQUARIUM

From then on, he was done
with the Creed of Constantinople
and climbing the ladder
to heaven on rungs
of celibate abbots and vicars,
done with novena
and Ave Marias
and on to theology
of rock-paper-scissors
with its new Eucharist
of conclusions: paper beats rock,
rock beats scissors,
scissors beat paper,
and claw beats tentacle
in this fuming aquatic struggle—
ex cathedra survival of the fittest
balling into pathos
where each of us
becomes at best
a type of hungry Caliban,
nothing but muscles
and tendons of lust.

RUMIESQUE PERHAPS

Told in thunderclap
by the holy will
of rain clouds

that sew such
bright evidence with
quilts of flowers,

there seems something
we ought to learn,
then learn to follow.

WALTER ANDERSON REGRETS KILLING A SEA TURTLE

What must it have been like,
dodging loony kisses, bearing all
the unintelligible Whitfield sounds
day after day while
you could still understand
Best Maugard's seven motifs in art—
whirling motion in a pine cone,
the occult of hovering gulls—
while your heart was out there
with the thunder and sunsets
of Horn Island paradise
where you could lie for hours
marveling at white sand swaths
of a copperhead, in waiting for dark
and the starlike stare around your camp
from some raccoon pantoum,
your heart there noting
our world's whole stage
in the pink eternity of a shell?
Though in the cleansing surf
of turquoise tide, through
waving sea oats of dream
your sin returns again and again
and again, lumbering
its inconsolable carapace bashed
in thoughtless, human moment
so that no iridescence of hummingbirds
needling between thistle

nor any cormorant's webbed revelation
might erase hapless, testudinal eyes,
which each night grew more
tortured, irreducible, Blakean.

THEORIES ON HOW VENUS DE MILO LOST HER ARMS

Truthful or not, let Chuck Berry tell it,
though she won the fight, it cost both her arms.
It's quite disarming that she'd show such grit,
fend off rivals for a handsome man's charms.

Her pleasantness belies alley cat ways
despite the viciousness bound with passion.
It's less fanciful if she spent her days
spinning thread, as some guess from her fashion,

if indeed the famous damage was done
during her more than a thousand years there
lost in a cave near the blue Aegean,
perhaps toy for tanned wastrels, then salt air.

What is it about the ungraspable:
van Gogh's ear, God's face, Mona Lisa's smile?

VINCENT'S FLOWERS

Islands unto ourselves,   as his *Blossoming Almond Branch*—

    a twig spreads white buds over a cerulean rim

  of rippled glass . . .

        then chattering crows in the yellow mania of wheat.

Even if the ear bobbing and paint eating were myth,

            fevered brushwork,

    revelations came and returned

in bursts of ecstasy and despair,

      style nodding to Rembrandt's.

    The torture of sunflowers starts—each stroke a barb

            on his canvas of nightmares,

but possessed by beauty.   A few hopeful blues

    painted to look like embers singeing, igniting.

      Fourteen Sunflowers in a Vase,

mostly in the carefree gold of Arles,

    his characteristic signature wrapped

around the vessel as proud and happy as that of a child.

        Sketch of a blossoming pear tree

                                    quickly labeled in French.

Vase with Daisies and Anemones—

                flowers like flowers instead of bonfires.

    Delacroix made him think about music

                          its shared harmonies with painting—

his drawing, *Garden with Sunflowers*,

                notes wildly escaping their staff.

      A fascination with Japan:

the people "live in nature as though they themselves were flowers"—

traces of ikebana—

finds himself in love again,   not with harlots

            and wine this time

                          nor the "gay colors" of Provence,

    but with the simple perfection of snow.

        To Émile Bernard, he tries to describe the lightninglike vicissitude

                    of plein-air painting—

hoping to sense color differently, to work more quickly.

                      Neither weather nor asylum at Saint-Rémy

    slows his force,   but allows

        night sky to be undiluted cobalt blue,

    stars to be like opals, emeralds, sapphires, and rubies.

Even in the break of painting *Augustine Roulin (La Berceuse)*,

her dress is the green of summer leaves,   her hair bun the red of roadside poppies,

        wallpaper behind her looks almost arabesque

    except for the idolatry of carnations and chrysanthemums.

              Pink Peach Trees:

"Probably the best landscape I have done . . . a frenzy of impastos . . .

        against a sky of glorious blue and white."

The irises, the irises,   remembering Doré,   *je me souviens*.

        He'd been reading Yoshimaro's *A New Book of Insects*, you see,

            become a student of rose beetles, cicadas, and butterflies

                circling the olive orchards at Saint-Rémy.

During quicksilver moments in asylum,

    writes to Theo of "disparate complementaries" and "juxtaposition,"

of purple and yellow flowers in Arles,

                              seeming "a Japanese dream,"

        details a painting with the sentiment of its parent:

    "the trunk of a pine violet-pink and then the grass

with white flowers and dandelions, a little rose tree

                and other tree trunks in the background."

        Beyond the cabarets of Paris,

lush impastos of peonies,   the fragrant throats of roses—

                flowers bring a degree of peace, and so too,

the influence of Courbet and Fantin-Latour.

                            The need of more money for paints

to keep up with his muse of blossoming orchards,

            the daimon mistrals swirling their sparkling insanity of petals.

    On about color,   challenges of the weather,

            on about "poplars and a very blue sky . . . and white flowers,

with a big yellow butterfly . . . a little garden with a fence

        of yellow reeds, and green bushes, and a flower bed."

Patches of ivy and periwinkles on Saint-Rémy's untended grounds, esoteric calyxes,

                and in the midst of marigolds, irises,

their heads like violet crowns.

Admirer of Hokusai, admirer of Renoir's roses—

in one of his sour moods, thinking,

Zut! This Gachet is no good to me except for the balm of his blooms.

Branches of Flowering Acacia, Vincent's silvery, abstracted leaves

and zigzag of golden flowers, seems most like his mind,

the struggle for dominion between dark and light.

Painting just a nest so viewers wouldn't be distracted

by any brilliant persuasion of birds—

hollow nights with women, the drinking and tiffs with Gauguin—

contented again for a while longer with his toy of utopian Japan,

the handy jumble of still-life motifs orbiting Gachet's rooms—

the globes of jutting blooms for *Japanese Vase with Roses and Anemones* in a style

not unlike Cezanne's,

despondent again over the scarcity of cornflowers in Provence.

"The sunflower is mine in a way": *Twelve Sunflowers in a Vase*,

Two Cut Sunflowers, One Upside Down, *Vase with Fourteen Sunflowers*—

"*les tons rompus et neutres* to harmonise brutal extremes"—

praises for Millet and Breton—

"an avalanche" of purple irises for the critic Isaäcson,

        yet another homage to the Japanese, Zola, and Cézanne.

Now it's the thatched roofs of Auvers,   their cottages curtained with blooms,

    to Theo on and on about Fontainebleau and wild boar

and larks and great oaks and rocks and even blades of grass.

With regard for Karl Bodmer and Pierre Loti,   those who reveled in nature's details.

        To Theo, the drudgery of sand and dust,

            wiping off paint-mired flies from canvases,

"absorbed" with the heath's hedges and thorns.

            Before studying Frans Hals, Rubens, Veronese, and Velazquez,

before Sisley, Monet, Renoir, and Degas,

            there's the utter surrender to color.

To sister Wil, the "blue blowballs . . . a bed of orange and yellow Africans . . .

    in the background, pink and lilac . . . also dark violet scabiosas . . .

red geraniums and sunflowers . . . a fig tree and an oleander and a vine,"

      still, "mere dabs of colour,"   painted "as in nature,"

"unbeautiful,"   "rather summery."

Vase with Poppies, Daisies, Cornflowers and Peonies,

                              much like his cosmos of stylized stars

tumbled and drifting,   a swirl

              of quasi-blue light.

                    "Beautiful like the Lesbos of Puvis de Chavannes,"

of the poisonous oleander   arranged in majolica beside Zola's *La Joie de vivre*,

        perhaps as talisman

                        against the cacophonous syllogism of crows

    always ready to explode from a field of startled wheat.

Auvers in bloom,   the daimon mistral—

        "brushwork firm and interwoven with feeling."

            "More like music . . . less like sculpture"

    in motifs of cornflowers and chrysanthemums, heliotrope and roses,

                poppies and geraniums.

Fritillarias in a Copper Vase,   "the curious relationship between

            one fragment of nature and another"—

        "*L'art c'est l'homme ajouté à la nature*"—

not in "the distance between the earth and moon . . . in studying Bismarck's policy,"

                but in seeing oneself as a blade of grass,

            untethered to the pilgrimage of Provençal daughters

wading through golden sunflowers   and poppies' blood red

to strew freshly cut though fading blooms over the bald soil of a tomb,

searching for the living among the dead.

IV

WEED

What easy, gluttonous bumble rolls
    through the dusty-rose desserts of clover

till I rip the cord of my mower
    for the first time each year.

Were it not for neighbors and vanity's sake,
    I'd simply let them be as beautiful as they are,

all the lawn daisies with their halos
    of white rays circling pastel heads

on near impossible to nip, supple
    green stems waving like standards

in early April's chilly breeze—
    and not just them, but the self-heal

and creeping buttercups, the star-shapes
    of ragwort, bumper crops of dandelion,

slender speedwell, or *Veronica filiformis*
    by its fancier handle, the purplish and white sprays

of bull thistle and wild carrot,
    a skulk of foxtail, velvet leaf, lady's thumb,

lamb's quarters, dead nettle,
    such orange wings of hawkweed,

the brilliant, brilliant yellow wood sorrel
    which must spring up overnight

like a fairy tale or Jonah's beloved
    gourd and seems too sacred to kill.

WASPS

Then without fail the wasps come,
    pheromonal ladies awakened

by our warming sun—
    bitter, syrupy-brown sprites,

maybe from under an elm stump,
    zooming in turbulent flight, as if notes

of Vaughan Williams or Delius.
    And again, they paper garrisons

around doorjambs and eaves
    till late spring or thereabouts,

again, enough already, back
    to the millenniums-old discord

over a trifling bite of fruit,
    when I reach to my poisons

which promise the upturned, hourglass
    bodies in graphic Saint Vitus's dance,

and that, at least for a season, there will be
    one less thing to harm the rest of my life.

A GUIDE FOR LISTENING TO MOCKINGBIRDS

Mimicry and improvising
is how they swing,
Mimus polyglottos,
from the Latin *mimus*, "a mimic,"
and the Greek *poluglottos*
meaning "many tongued."

Tribes bore witness, calling it
cencontlatolly, meaning
"four hundred tongues,"
and *hushi balbaka*,
"bird that speaks
a foreign language,"
the Cherokees going so far
as to feed mockingbird hearts
to children to help them
learn to speak.

Though Anglophiles thought
the songsters little more
than a poor relation
to their Old World nightingale,
Audubon held that nightingales,
compared to mockingbirds,
were at best an opening act.

But forget about
Harper Lee's musing
their lack of sassiness,
that only the gentlest notes
spring from their souls.

Remember, part of their name
comes from *muccare*, that is,
to "wipe one's nose,"
or "mock"—long
a symbol of scorn.

Why, with these own eyes,
I've watched the almost
lavender darts of their bodies
blitz hawks and farm cats
and squirrels, then too,
I've heard them hid
in the treacle
of a honeysuckle shrub
even making fun
of our car alarms
and so much other
of our material world.

THE LOVE LIFE OF MOSS

There's so much more to it
    than the cool, spongy swell of chartreuse,

teal, and viridian. Though
    you would hardly guess along

a nearly biblical stream,
    cloaked by the prayers of redbirds

and rich confessions of thrush,
    everywhere fed from canticles of soft

sunlight, that beneath bare,
    artless feet such freaky, alien stuff

is going on among sphagnum,
    apple, haircap or whatever, as male

antheridiums grow ripe and damp
    then burst toward girl archegoniums,

where at last together, deep
    in the heart of the egg, they become

long, erect, and continue a lot
    of other, unpronounceable things

with mouths and "teeth" through
    a swirling Kamasutra of spores,

all under our very toes, so to speak.

FLOWER MOON

By such luminance
I could see grass spiders
skate over a sheet of light
or find jangling herons
who've returned out back
from their diurnal ponds
to roost in dim branches
of hickory and ash.

Even, it seems,
just a few years ago,
such a spectacle would've drawn
me like the tides, but now
in this age of different concerns,
without the plump appetites
for muscadines, to taste
the world day and night . . .

and so, I can't tell my friend
in California, when she calls
and wants to know if I too
had waded under the flood
of our year's brightest moon,
anything other than
I had only watched it
for a while from inside.

INTERNECINE

Whenever I discover
them raising others
of those ugly, troublesome
temples over the yard
or somehow breaking the code
of closed windows, solving
the maze of one's plumbing
or mapping cracks
in the foundation slab,
searching for their grail
of sugar, a lost crumb
of ham, they are always
consummate, harmonious strings
being played on a psaltery
or harp, every passage
colored by rote and any
forced improvisations
worked out ahead of time.

Yet there is another term,
internecine, that's been used
remarking ants, perhaps
first, if not only, by Thoreau—
a word that sounds as if
it also could be to do with music,
like *intermezzo* or *agitato*—
as near Walden, he witnessed
the tangle of red against black,
black against red, shredding
feelers and legs, lopping
heads without mercy or end,

so much so it seemed the war
that began and raged
from Heaven had spilled
onto this band of brothers,
even unto them.

DESTROYING ANGEL

We're obliged
to be seduced
by any of *belladonna's*
four beautiful syllables,
a mystery deep
in the purple
of her innocent-looking cup,
so that we would
chance our hearts
to survive.
But this amanita,
nourished by death, named
in Old Testament fashion,
sounds wrathful
from the start,
looks the part too,
though svelte under
that bitter umbrella,
and as bright
as those once were
who first fell
from heaven.

DUET

Anything miraculous, we try to rationalize,
to explain in terms of less thrilling science.

For example, I give you male and female
plain-tailed wrens living in the bamboo forests

of Ecuador, and whose wooing is this synchronous
antiphony, still such an Edenic bond, yet also

strained through the flesh to suggest
that it's no more than enough polynomials

and grammar-compliant sentences evolved
to form the birds' own combinatorial language—

indeed, the same as any two humans learning
to tango, rowing a boat in rhythm, or having good sex,

rather than to just hear all things
of heaven and earth in harmony again,

and for the moment, singing.

DRAGONFLIES HUNTING

Oftentimes behind
    a lawn mower's fire,
        or just after summer showers,

their pattern glides
    in the relished gold
        and sapphire of amulets,

very art nouveau,
    out of nowhere
        each tandem-winged one's

chitinous shell
    a glistening fighter plane
        dive-bombing our yards—

all of them fresh off
    eerie years of aquatic training
        as predators, yet still before

the hearts and wheels
    of mating flight, from
        nymphs to sunlit hawkers

now ready for
    their last ravenous days,
        they hover and dart to seize

small distractions of movement
    through grass or air as only
        such omniscient eyes could freeze.

LIVE BAIT

All the mom-and-pop stores
advertising their sausage biscuits
and fish bait with equal pride
recall mornings when I,
with maybe one other boy,
mined the whole rich earth
for night crawlers and crickets,
then set out with our Zebco rods
and empty lard buckets for creels,
both of us along the way
thieves among berry vines.

At the day's spot would come
the baiting I probably hated
even back then. It wasn't that
any of them cried audibly
or kicked or squirmed
more than expected as I looped
my hook through and through
its body, but that each one
needed to stay alive as long
as possible for the rest of it,

to go on struggling, tempting,
after being arced and sunk
below the skim of a pond,
dangled like Job before Satan,
at the lightning gape of crappie

and perch, at the lightning gape
of bluegill and bream, sometimes
reeled out at the limit of hope,
sometimes nibbled beyond use.

Only if I caught something
did their lives seem less in vain,
which in itself was still
a cruel sort of irony,
save for a while our sharing
the quiet shrines
of sycamores and willows
casting our sun-dappled path.

COTTONMOUTH

In deeper, to a kingdom
    of tangled branches,
through morning's annoying orb of spiders,
    we would at times happen upon it

looped on a cool creek bank
    under snake doctors' darting charms,
amid the rising singing
    by bluebirds and finches,

and then somewhere
    along glistened moss pads,
we would also find our perfect wand,
    long enough for foolishly seasoned

among boys and men alike
    to stay just out of reach
while teasing the sour maw
    till it opened up, wider, even wider still

to show us its cottony deviltry,
    that blinding white light so many
of the salvaged dying claim to have seen
    and began moving toward.

MONTEGO BAY

From the verandah of my hotel,
I watched storm clouds roll in
as charged and dark as the adolescent boy
still plodding his way to the tip
of a rocky shoreline, paying no mind
to the bloom of lightning
nearing the surf
nor to my silent petition
for some older brother or cousin
to whoop and curse him indoors—

now wishing I was the sort
to shuck decorum and cry out to him
all my warnings from the wisdom
of ages, that he should save himself
to see morning's cool striations
of teal and indigo waters
sweeping the bay again, to witness
a sparkle of swirling white gulls
tossed through the clear like glitter,
to watch a local mug
for some tourist's souvenir,
and for seeing again
the charming putto
who will toddle a few steps
from his mother's dozing grace
to wet the ivory sand.

What need now to say anything
of once being so young
and commending my own life
to tolerant angels
while dipped naked and neck-deep
in the shady, moccasin-rich creeks
of a Mississippi bottom,
sometimes even with thunder
rumbling up the horizon?

THE GOLIATH BIRD-EATING SPIDER

Under an ancient-looking prop, it hides,
especially from the young Spanish boy
peering, straining to fathom its great size.
Behind the haunted glass, there seems a ploy
to suspend our mystery while it bides,
covered by moss and web and scraps of wood.
A placard of its reputation bids
we image what would scoff it, is its food;
the Philistine who cursed God without care—
proclaiming it king of all arachnids,
that other spiders should gaze and despair!
But its terrarium is just as small
as ants' or roaches' exhibited there,
showing mostly, even the mighty fall.

THE MUD DAUBER AND THE MOTH

Fixed to my window,
a thunder-gray moth slumbers
seeming yet under the sugary influence
after an all-nighter in full cups
of honeysuckle and moonflower,
occasionally twitching a furled proboscis,
shuffling some glittery dust
off its doubled frenulum,
like the way we might suck our teeth
or turn over in sleep, oblivious
to another God-blue morning upon us.

One wonders if there will be strife
as a glossy mud dauber
flits in humming her work song,
her jaws filled with clay and spittle
to claim a corner of the same high pane.

Then just before clouds thicken
for a hazy shower, I finish rereading
a former student's poem, that I think
is to do with hunger, and begin
weighing what to answer her
about a failing marriage.

When our rain clears as quickly
as it came, I glance back, perhaps
hoping for bright allegory
from the wasp or moth, each of whom,
if not helping the other's cause,
is at least minding its own beeswax,
showing what we always have to give
even when we have nothing to offer.

A HUNTER WITH A 23½-POUND WILD TURKEY HEADS TOWARD HIS BOAT NEAR BIG ISLAND ON THE MISSISSIPPI RIVER

after a photograph of Arkansas Publicity and Parks Commission

Leaving us now, in tan
huntsman's coat and cap,
arrested in midstep,
shotgun shouldered
and feathered prize
fanned across his back,
the rolling skiff,
some bleached driftwood,
and a barely visible
scumbling of trees just
above the water's sheen
seem all that are in his sights.

And yet, there at banks
that are neither tossed
nor driven, still
we perhaps wonder
if our hunter
is considering
a new recipe,
the best taxidermist,
or troubles he left before
shoving off this morning
into the river's
old nonchalance.

DEER CROSSING

Early one evening in summer or autumn—
    probably autumn—along Mississippi 304,

I learned the difference between desire
    and calling. And though I don't recollect

enough of the rest of the day to flesh out
    any life-changing epistle,

afterward I couldn't forget that line
    from a William Stafford poem

resounding, "I thought hard for us all."
    Even without the infamy of any yellow warning

with an antlered silhouette launched in space,
    I simply knew every lane should slow down

when first the doe appeared bounding
    toward and over a pasture fence, then

another just as lithe, and the steady buck
    chasing them both. Surviving every

radiant mangling coming from our direction
    and then the familiar grasses of the median,

the prima deer began to mix metaphors
    as her pointe hooves hit the next slippery stage,

missed their jeté and sent her skidding
    on her flank like a base runner narrowly

ducking a tag from drivers who refused to stop.
    Apostolic in their creed,

their fearlessness of uncertainty, they kept the same stride
    even after witnessing such a thin escape,

each deer breaking through in turn, knowing nothing
    but a promise, and that on the other side.

THUSNESS

Through autumn's early light
slanting under curtains
over the kitchen sink,
a spider, verily minuscule,
who somehow stole in
like a thief in the night,

creeps the windowsill
across each stroke
of brightness then shade
then brightness then shade,
as if on a great commission
from, dare I say, its soul.

With nothing more
or less to think of
for the moment,
I wonder if it loves,
or even has to love God.

And if so, is this homage
only due when somewhere
a glassy beetle
or nectar-fat candlefly
hangs in its faithful web?

FORECAST

Meanwhile, out there
among mottled shadows
and just beyond October's
first glints of gold,
crows are cosigning
the weatherman's prediction,
nagging that I should've risen earlier
to make a start on the yard,
that lying in bed
contemplating the arc
of one's life is wasted time
better spent raking
the latest harvest
of sweet gum balls,
or perhaps studying etchings
by Dürer and Mellan,
or simply watching
the Cooper's hawk
hovered over lunch
beneath a chokecherry,
then flying for the nearby fence
and squirting a silky dénouement
before taking off
toward sheltering groves
to wait out the certainty of rain.

REVELATION

What is it you've looked at
    that quickened your next breaths,

left you beholden, stunned
    with its essence in the earth:

perhaps a homely buzzard,
    of all things, unafraid and staying

high on the wing while buffeted
    about like a plume of soot

against rolling storm clouds;
    that glittering carp swum

from its cover of amber water,
    flashing now and then

along the clear shallow,
    so at home even without our air;

symbiosis made flesh
    as morning's white herons

shop a low river
    and fringes of swamp pink;

or, just making their flight into open field
    beneath November's yellow canopy,

the suite of honey-colored, tined,
    rut-ready bucks

glimpsed through the lens
    of such golden noon light?

WINTER FIELD WHITE WITH SNOW GEESE

I'd thought to entice my students
    with Baudelaire's indulgences in absinthe

and his mulatto mistress, though none of them
    ever give a sonnet about anything

at 8:00 a.m. in a cold, fluorescent room.
    What an anachronism I must seem

drifting back by rote, still loving
    the lives of those from centuries ago, only I

waltzing among dusty museums
    of synesthesia and empire as if

through a tableau vivant
    before their drowsing eyes.

But nearing yesterday's bland fields,
    there's suddenly now such a blizzard

of honking and descending splendor
    that I recall a story about sacred geese

kept in the Temple of Juno, how
    their startled racket supposedly alerted

sleeping Rome before Gauls invaded,
    thus saving the day as it were—

and for me, my own segue
   out of the world's apathy

as these many thousand white blessings
   offer their random seconds of beauty.

WORLD WITHOUT END

On a slow steam train to Snowdonia,
zephyrs of white spores swirled around
every railroad car, landscape sauntered past
with its bellwether rams and contented ewes,
its painterly cattle mirrored in streams—
all paying homage to hills clouded
with heather and amethyst horizon.

Across a challenge of trestles, we moved
between dromedary ridges pinched
from green and greener gorges
that reminded me of kindred trees
thousands of miles away, where
I'm chosen to witness a rosy moth
fill itself with the sweetness
of flowers, and to hear the whistle
of a rust-red she hawk, proud
over her speckled future in a nest
haunting woods near where we live,

where on occasion, matrimonial owls
glide moonlit from thickets of fireflies,
where raccoons and deer share our yard
having grown so used to each other,
as if part of Hicks's *Peaceable Kingdom*,
in which wolf and lambs cuddle together,
leopard and goat lie shoulder to shoulder.

Before passing through a tunnel,
an ironic porter emerged, looking and sounding
more dead than alive, pushing his rickety cart

of choices among coffee, tea, and muffins,
then wailing to the aisle and windows
rather than to any of us, "Refreshments . . .
refreshments . . . refreshments,"
till I imagined him young again,
commuting past morning quarries,
if not to this then some other job,
but with a baritone full of promise that
made travelers hungry instead of sad.

And at their little beginner's cottage
folded in burgundy roses, was the bride
whom he could still make blush,
who earnestly wanted to know
how each day had gone,
if he had spilled anything, or if
anyone famous had been aboard.

But I understood how such halcyon time
could have passed like a breath into this,
passed from a young poet's dim prayer
to find some bright cosmology
in the crowning tuft of a quail,
to now and unhurried cows, easy brooks,
the kaleidoscope of afternoon shadows
continuing as they always have.

Perhaps as I'd been watching sea birds
hover then land atop roofs in Caernarfon,
memory returns the gull who swooped
on my friend's lunch in Alberta,
and before long, the unbearable truth
that none of this would tarry, not the porter,
not I, nor even the young of the hawk
back home, yet everything goes on.

Acknowledgments

The author offers grateful acknowledgment to the following publications, in which some of the poems herein originally appeared, sometimes in a different form:

Arkansas International: "Winter Field White with Snow Geese"

Arkansas Review: "Auspice," "Remembering My Mother Cleaning Fish"

Briar Cliff Review: "Prophecy"

Chronicles: "Covenant," "Lenten"

Louisiana Literature: "Forecast"

Naugatuck River Review: "Among Other Things, My Father Teaches Me How to Mow Grass"

Poem: "Flower Moon," "Live Bait," "Weed"

Poetry South: "Four-leaf Clovers in Bibles," "Revelation"

Red Rock Review: "In the Beginning, Audubon"

Saint Katherine Review: "Duet"

Snowy Egret: "Praise"

Windhover: "Heaven and Earth"

This book was set in Mrs. Eaves, designed by Slovak typographer Zuzana Licko in 1996. The founder of the renowned firm, Émigré Graphics, Licko decided with this font to take on the challenge of re-interpreting the classic Baskerville typeface, originally created in the 1750s. Mrs. Eaves has been described as sometimes "awkward" but also possessing "an undefined quality that resonates with people." It is named after Sarah Eaves, originally William Baskerville's housekeeper, whom he later married.

This book was designed by Ian Creeger, Jim Tedrick, and Gregory Wolfe. It was published in hardcover, paperback, and electronic formats by Slant Books, Seattle, Washington.

The cover image is a detail from *Solitude*, 30 x 40 inches, oil on canvas, 2007 by the author of this book, Claude Wilkinson.

www.ingramcontent.com/pod-product-compliance
Lightning Source LLC
Chambersburg PA
CBHW051700040426
42446CB00009B/1221